a clowder of CATS

Nickolas Muray

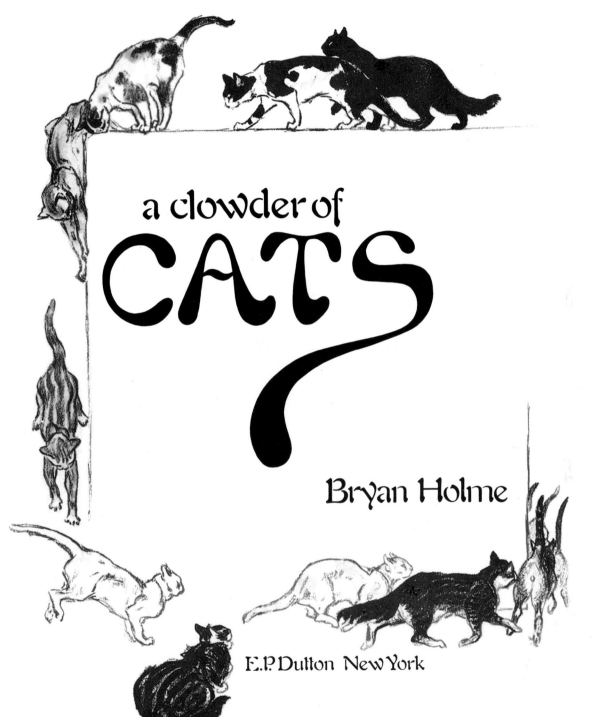

a clowder of
CATS

Bryan Holme

E.P. Dutton New York

First published, 1986, in the
United States by E. P. Dutton

Copyright © 1985 by The Herbert Press
Copyright under the Berne Convention

All rights reserved.

No part of this publication may be
reproduced or transmitted in any form
or by any means, electronic or mechanical,
including photocopy, recording or any
information storage and retrieval system
now known or to be invented, without
permission in writing from the publisher,
except by a reviewer who wishes to quote
brief passages in connection with a review
written for inclusion in a magazine,
newspaper or broadcast.

Published in the United States by
E. P. Dutton,
2 Park Avenue, New York, N.Y. 10016.

Library of Congress Catalog Card
Number: 85–71398

ISBN: 0–525–24381–X

First published in Great Britain 1985 by
The Herbert Press Limited
Designed by Bryan Holme
Jacket design by Pauline Harrison

Printed and bound in Hong Kong by
South China Printing Co.
Published simultaneously in Canada by
Fitzhenry & Whiteside Limited, Toronto
CUSA
10 9 8 7 6 5 4 3 2 1
First edition
FRONTISPIECE Photograph by W.
Suschitzky
TITLE PAGE Drawing by T.-A. Steinlen
from *The Studio*

Foreword

The author wishes to take this opportunity once more to thank most sincerely his friends in the world of art and photography as well as the publishers, museums and galleries who throughout the years have been so generous in allowing their treasures to be reproduced in 'The Studio' and Studio Books – the latter for many years being an imprint of The Viking Press in New York. Most of the illustrations in this book are reprinted from The Studio and Studio books, including works from his own volume, *Cats and Kittens* which has been out of print for over forty years. He also wishes to thank all the various and very dear members of his family, as well as Yvonne McHarg, Mary Velthoven, and David and Brenda Herbert for their assistance.

Franz Huld 1908

Introduction

Many readers may wonder how the word 'Clowder' came to be used in the title of this book. Apart from the necessity of finding a different sounding title from any used on the many hundreds of earlier tributes to this very special creature, there was the more interesting idea of reviving the correct yet all but forgotten word for an assemblage of cats.

'A Clowder of Cats' does state, and sound as if it states, exactly what the book contains – not cats alive and rough and tumbling – how nice if it could – but an assemblage of cats as seen by artists and photographers, each expert in making them appear not only alive but graceful, amusing and otherwise at their irresistible best.

But the word 'Clowder' would never have entered my head – and pretty certainly not my publisher's either – had I not happened to fall heir to *The Academy of Armory and Blazon*, a book on heraldry written and illustrated by a distant ancestor, Randle Holme, while he was, if the title page is to be believed, 'Gentleman Sewer in Extra-ordinary to His Majesty King Charles II'. The work – it must have been his life work – was finished in the reign of William and Mary and published in 1688.

It was in this book that I remembered having discovered, buried among thousands of entries, lists of terms for birds, insects and animals 'when they are in companyes'. While struggling with the olde English, not to mention the type face, I started wondering why it was that some of these 'companyes', such as a 'pack' of hounds, for example, or a 'swarm' of bees, a 'covey' of partridges, a 'shoal' of fishes and even a 'flight' of doves, have remained part of our everyday language, while others like a 'gaggle' of geese, an 'exalting' of larks, a 'slowth' of bears, a 'tripp' of goats and a 'pace' of asses haven't.

By the way, Holme also lists a 'swrednes ' of apes. Plainly, the typesetter was guilty of dropping an 'h', misplacing the 'w' and

T.-A. Steinlen

T.-A. Steinlen

couldn't for the life of him find a second 's' in his font. Unless, perhaps, 'swrednes' was correct then as 'a shrewdness of apes' is now. I doubt it.

For the record, Holme allows that a gathering of cats is also rightly called a 'kindle' or 'wauling' of cats, that a cat 'maueth' and 'purreth', and when giving birth to its young 'kittleth'.

But most authorities, including Hodgkin in *Proper Terms*, stay with 'clowder', a word to be found in some dictionaries and deriving very possibly from 'cluster'.

© H. A. Frink

Photo: John Mills Jr

A Clowder of Cats

A home without a cat, and a well-fed
well petted and properly revered cat,
may be a perfect home, *perhaps*, but
how can it prove its title?

Mark Twain

The Cheshire Cat, drawn by John
Tenniel for Lewis Carroll's *Alice
in Wonderland*

Surely no one really believes that a cat has nine lives, even if he says
he does – like the English author, Oswald Barron who, writing in
Day In and Day Out about his own beloved pet, observed 'that every
pussy has nine lives is a truth not to be questioned'.

Perhaps in the land of fairy tales? Yet even there, *Puss in Boots* had
but one life, *The White Cat* two or, pushing it a little, three, and as
for the Cheshire Cat in *Alice in Wonderland*, it had vanished before
anyone found out.

But, if there wasn't a grain of truth in old sayings like 'cats have
nine lives, onions and women seven skins' or 'curiosity killed the cat
and satisfaction brought it back', how did such ideas ever take hold
of the public's imagination in the first place?

Be that as it may, centuries ago in Europe it was little short of
miraculous that the cat – with one life or even with nine lives –
managed to survive the most outrageous atrocities any animal ever
suffered at the hands of man; a sorry subject to be touched on again
later. And then from the depths of degradation, regarded with suspicion, dread, hatred, *Felis catus* gradually found its way back up the
social ladder rung by rung, to be tolerated, looked upon with indif-
ference, then admired once more. Finally, puss knew it could curl up
in someone's welcoming lap, *when* it wanted to, and purr in the sun-
shine of human adulation.

Owners know how a cat will often sit quietly to observe and to
meditate, with eyes seemingly focused on the far beyond. Probably

this is why it is often said that to look into the sphinx-like eyes of a cat is to sense eternity. Partly for this reason some people have always feared cats, finding them too aloof and mysterious for comfort, while others succumb endlessly to their fascination. In ancient Egypt, where the cat was named 'mau', meaning 'to see', the latter seems to have been particularly true.

From all accounts, it was there, in Egypt at least 4,000 years ago, and very possibly untold centuries earlier, that a new, small breed of cat was evolved from larger species that roamed the African wilds. The Egyptians developed, trained and kept petting the little creature until it was finally invited indoors where, except for a few freakish incidents in history, it has lived happily ever after.

In some respects the story of the domestic cat does read like a fairy tale. To begin with, in Egypt, fortune so smiled on it that, had the cat been human, we wouldn't have hesitated to refer to it as one of those lucky creatures born with a silver spoon in its mouth.

After all, to be pampered and given the run of the house, to accompany the master as a retriever on fabulous hunting forays along the Nile (this we see in wall paintings dated around 1400 BC), to be ap-

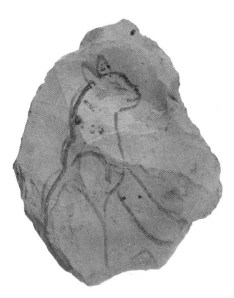

Egyptian cat. From a sketch on flaked limestone *c.* 1500–1100 BC (*Fitzwilliam Museum, Cambridge*)

Mutsa with his Family and Cat. Drawing from *The Manners and Customs of the Ancient Egyptians* by Sir J. Gardner Wilkinson, John Murray 1878

9

Cat in the manner of an Egyptian bronze by Heath Robinson (detail) for 'Puss in Boots' in *Perrault's Complete Fairy Tales*, Dodd, Mead & Company Inc.

plauded for indulging in what was its favourite pastime anyway – pouncing on mice – and then, crowning it all, to find itself by virtue of its master's religious beliefs invited into the sacred precincts of temples where its very image was bowed down to and worshipped as divine: what more could any animal possibly ask? Obviously it was having the most heavenly time on earth.

As far as history books tell, no period ever did equal those golden years in Egypt, until perhaps the present day when, enshrined not on a pedestal in a temple but on the drawing-room couch, the cat, in the eyes of its more passionate fans, is again completely and utterly divine.

To begin with, where else but in cats, these fans ask, can such a variety of fabulous furs be found? Soft as silk, short haired or long, snow white, cream or black, lilac-hued, bronze or tan, marmalade or chocolate, smokey blue or silver gray, chinchilla or tortoiseshell,

plain, shaded, striped, bi-coloured or spotted. And along with all this come a wide variety of countenances, colours of eyes, and voices.

The real 'cat's whiskers' to many fanciers are the hybrids originating in exotic lands afar; Persia, Turkey, the Himalayas, and Siam – where the cat enjoyed the status of royalty.

'Pussy was a goddess in old Egypt', wrote Oswald Barron, 'and she has never forgotten it. Old incense perfumes her soft fur. A goddess in exile, she exacts honour as any queen who has lost a realm but will have her court and its courtiers.'

Cat with bow. Artist unknown
1908

Drawing by Randolph Caldecott
from *The House that Jack Built*,
Frederick Warne & Co., London

It is not unknown still for her majesty the cat to be adorned by an adoring owner with a collar or necklace of simulated pearls, rubies, emeralds or diamonds, and more often with a ribbon – as was Jenny Lind's blue-ribboned black cat to whom she sang so sweetly. But never, we hope, in recent history have the ears or nose of a cat been pierced to be hung with rings of gold or silver as were some of those depicted in ancient Egyptian bronzes.

So treasured was the cat in Egypt – for its part in freeing the country's vast granaries from vermin as well as for more esoteric reasons – that two strict laws were introduced for the animal's preservation. One of them made it a crime for anyone to take a cat abroad – which, human nature being what it is, simply meant that foreign fanciers were all the more anxious – and determined – to get one, by crook if not by hook. At one time the price paid for a good Egyptian cat along the upper shores of the Mediterranean was evidently tempting enough for numbers of sailors, particularly Phoenicians, to take the risk of smuggling them out of the country. Aware of this illegal traffic, officials were sent abroad to try to retrieve smuggled cats, *and* their kittens.

Most of these cats found their way to Europe via Greece, where Aesop was to associate the cat with the Goddess Venus and the feminine form in general. As this association stuck through the centuries, the word 'catty' arose in relation to those members of the fairer sex prone upon occasion, and when aroused by others, to making their claws felt through the exchange of barbs. Later, cats were also imported in increasing numbers through the thriving port of Venice, which was to become renowned for its orange cats. Of these, two later descendants may have served as models for the Tiepolo drawing now treasured in London's Victoria and Albert Museum.

A poem, based very loosely – some say probably not at all – on an ancient document, and much treasured in cat lore, was written by Graham Tomson in the nineteenth century. The verses tell of the fair Greek maiden, Arsinoë, whose craving for a handsome Egyptian cat became so passionate that she threw over her beau for refusing to

12

fetch her one and embraced another who promised he would, and evidently did. In the last verse of the poem, the rejected suitor lamented:

> A little lion, small and dainty sweet
> > (for such there be!)
> With sea-grey eyes and softly-stepping feet,
> > She prayed for me.
> For this through lands Egyptian far away
> > She bade me pass;
> But in an evil hour I said her nay:
> > And now, alas!
> Far-travelled Nicias hath wooed and won Arsinoë
> With gifts of furry creatures white and dun
> > From over-sea.

Drawing from a Greek vase 4C BC

It is possible to suppose that after Alexander the Great's occupation of Egypt in 333 BC the laws against exporting cats might have been relaxed, at least to the extent that a Greek soldier or sailor could sneak the occasional cat home, even if the practice was still against the local law.

The other relevant Egyptian law called for the death of anyone found guilty of killing a cat. So strictly was this enforced that, were a person to observe a cat lying dead or dying by the wayside, he would give it the widest berth to allay any possible suspicion of his being involved.

A famous story that makes its way into most cat histories revolves around the death of one of these sacred creatures. In 50 BC when the country was occupied by the Romans, the Egyptian government was particularly anxious to remain on the best of footings with Rome. It was then that a Roman soldier, according to one theory, accidentally stumbled and fell on a cat and squashed the poor creature to death. It's hard to imagine a normally agile cat not darting out of the soldier's way in time. However, the accident apparently did happen – if

Mosaic from Pompeii (National Museum, Naples)

Drawing for 'The Crooked Man's crooked cat' in *Ring o' Roses* by Leonard Leslie Brooke, Frederick Warne & Co., London

indeed it was an accident – the cat was killed, the Roman did it and the wrath of the natives upon hearing of the incident was such that mobs raced to the spot, set upon the soldier and finished him off. At least one historian has said that the incident caused a war. Others claim that diplomacy finally prevailed.

There is, alas, very little mention of the cat in the heydays of either Greece or Rome, which means we must make the most of the few snippets that have fallen our way.

In 270 BC, Theocritus remarked that 'all cats like a cushioned couch' thus informing us of the presence of the animal in Greece at the time, and suggesting the comfort it was afforded. It is tempting to try to complete the picture by imagining the design of the couch on which Theocritus must have seen his or someone else's cat lying, the colour and weave of the fabric, what the room looked like, and, naturally, the kind and colour of the cat.

Another fragment is found in an Italian document dated 75 AD which tells of a certain Aulus Pudens, an Umbrian serving as a Centurion in Pannonia, who was in the habit of sending gifts to his 'sponsor' in Rome. Two such offerings were 'golden orioles and green woodpeckers' which Aulus chose rather than 'Pannonian cats'. Why Aulus favoured the birds and whether any feline from Pannonia ever made it to Rome as a change of pace is not recorded.

Among Roman treasures that have come down to us through the ages is the famous mosaic of a cat unearthed in the ruins of Pompeii. To compare this with the photograph taken by Edward Weston in California during the 1940s is to observe how throughout the centuries, the look of the animal hasn't changed an iota. Indeed, were there not 2,000 or so years lying between the dates of the two images, it wouldn't be at all hard to believe the cat in Weston's photograph was the model for the mosaic.

Although the Romans went so far as to honour the cat as a symbol of liberty, and placed an image of it at the foot of their Goddess of

T.-A. Steinlen

Photograph from *The Cats of Wildcat Hill* by Edward Weston, Duell, Sloan & Pearce, New York

15

The Great Cat Ra, carving off the head of Apophis, god of darkness and chaos. Copy of the 1300 BC fresco in the tomb of Sennedjem in Egypt (Metropolitan Museum of Art, New York)

Liberty in the temple dedicated to her in 300 BC, they failed to understand the religious extremes to which the Egyptians went in revering the cat.

'And not only the Egyptians were fools of this kind,' one cynical Roman wrote, 'but the Arabians also worshipped the cat for a God, and when the cat died, they mourned as much for her as for the father of the family, shaving their hair from their eyelids, and carrying the beast to the temple'.

The principal feline deity worshipped by the Egyptians was Bast, or Bastet, also known as Bubastis and Pasht. It's rather nice to believe, as many experts do, that a corruption of Pasht gave us our word 'puss'.

Revered as 'The lady of the moon', patroness of 'Love, fertility and joy', Bast, like other animal and bird-headed Egyptian deities, was depicted as a standing figure dressed as a human but with the head of a cat.

Worship of Bast is believed to have dated from at least 4000 BC, reaching its height around 1500 BC when thousands of pilgrims, often wearing amulets in the form of the cat goddess, poured into the sacred city of Bubastis to take part in the annual festival in and around the beautiful temple. That Bast's influence continued long afterwards is suggested by existing bronzes of her, dated around 500 BC and later.

The other noted feline deity was a tom cat, the Great God Ra, known to us in illustrations dating around 1300 BC. In these, Ra is depicted wearing a pious smile while effortlessly carving off the head of its arch enemy, the serpent Apophis, God of Darkness and Chaos. The Egyptian belief in the transmigration of souls made it perfectly logical for artists to represent animals executing the tasks associated with humans before their reincarnation.

As Egypt's greatness diminished, so did the influence of its Gods, which were soon to be all but forgotten. Meanwhile the roles of certain of its deities were being assumed by those of other civilizations, notably in the mythologies of Greece and Northern Europe. Thus it was that the diminishing role of Bast in Egypt, specifically, as the goddess of love and fertility, came to be assumed by Venus in Greece and in northern Europe by Freya, a goddess also rather ominously known for her mysterious connections with the dead. And thereby hangs the cats' most sorrowful tale.

In the fifteenth century, seemingly out of nowhere, the cult of Freya was revived in Germany. Unlike Bast, the Norse goddess Freya was not cat-headed; instead, she commanded a team of what must have been the sturdiest cats in history who, at her bidding, carried her in a chariot across the starry skies.

This Freya cult was to involve innocent cats, first in hundreds, then in thousands. In preparation for each meeting, held in some consecrated spot, the female worshippers of Freya would round up any hapless cats they could lay their hands on and bundle them off to take a most unwilling part in their wildly orgiastic rites. These 'over-zealous devotees of Freya', writes Alleine Dodge, 'were probably largely responsible for the folk traditions of the 'Witches' Sabbath and Walpurgis Night, which led to the witchcraft persecutions of the sixteenth, seventeenth and eighteenth centuries'.

That the church should be horrified and preach against the worship of the heathen Freya was more than to be expected. But then in 1484 came a frightful edict from Rome. All Freya followers were ordered by Pope Innocent VIII to be rounded up and burned as witches. The fate that befell cats, who were now represented as the familiars of witches if not of the devil himself, was even worse. Torturing cats in ways too ghastly to describe, prior to their slaughter, was encouraged and soon became the sport of the ignorant masses.

Things reached a point of such madness that a woman had only to own a cat to find herself held as a likely suspect and prepare for her end accordingly. Before the holocaust was over, it is reported, by one source at least, that some ten per cent of the female population of Germany had been burned at the stake. Obviously a far, far greater proportion of the cat population must have disappeared the same way. All this because of Freya! Although surely a proper deity would never have willed such atrocities had she, indeed, ever existed, let alone

Egyptian cat-headed goddess Bast
(or Bastet), bronze 7C BC
(Fitzwilliam Museum, Cambridge)

Flying witch with cat. Silhouette
by Jaye Holme

Cat and witch (detail) by Kuniyoshi

known what was going on, there must have been thousands who thought Freya no goddess, but an un-honest-to-God witch.

From those dark days on, the familiar of the witch in folk and fairy tale continued to be a cat, customarily a black cat ready at her mistress's croak or cackle to travel aloft with her as she took to the skies on a broomstick. Sometimes when a black cat was seen alone, particularly at night, it was feared that it might be a witch like the nasty creature in the fairy tale *Jorinda and Joringel* who sometimes appeared as a cat, sometimes as an owl.

Precisely when some of these fanciful tales originated will never be established. They were passed on orally from generation to generation, undoubtedly gaining a new twist from one born story-teller or another along the way, until Charles Perrault and the Comtesse d'Aulnoy in France and the Brothers Grimm in Germany started to write down stories that some of the old folks remembered from their childhood days.

Witches with familiars. 17C woodcut, artist unknown

Illustration for *Mother Goose: Old
Nursery Rhymes* by Arthur Rackham,
(courtesy Barbara Edwards, daughter of the artist)

18

Photo: Martin Munkacsi

In fact, as well as fiction, continuing superstitions about witches, black magic, demons and familiars resulted in renewed persecutions. In England in the 1650s, during the Commonwealth, sixty women apparently were condemned and burned as witches. In Presbyterian Scotland, too, for nearly another hundred years, merely owning a cat, particularly a black cat, could be enough for a woman to be suspected of communication with the devil and thus end up in flames. Across the Atlantic, in Massachusetts, the Salem witch trials took place, and in South Carolina similar charges of witchcraft continued on and off until shortly before the turn of the nineteenth century.

Meanwhile, of course, there were always those who loved cats, a notable example being Cardinal Richelieu, who surrounded himself with cats in France. When he died in 1642, he left pensions to fourteen of these pets, as well as goodly sums to their caretakers. In the following century, Louis XIII, while he was still Dauphin, interceded with his father Henry IV to abolish, at least once, the ghastly custom of flinging live cats into the fire at the feast of St John – a practice his son, the later Louis XIV (to his lasting shame), was guilty not only of condoning but of actually indulging in himself. He was, apparently, the last French king to do so.

Throughout history the fate of the black cat varied as much as the

T.-A. Steinlen

19C woodcut, unknown
English artist

'Black Cat' by John Rawlings

Illustration by Aubrey Beardsley for Edgar Allan Poe's *The Black Cat*, Herbert S. Stone and Company, Chicago, 1894–5

flip of a coin. It was that chancey – one day tails up, the black cat spelled good luck, another day, another flip, tails down, it spelled bad luck. Much depended, of course, on the time, the place and the person, and in which direction the wind of superstition blew.

In 393 AD Aristophanes was, it seems, the first to record that 'if a cat crosses your path it's a sign of bad luck' – a belief ailurophiles have been saying nonsense to ever since. Aristophanes didn't say 'a black cat', but as the superstition continued through centuries, 'black' would sometimes creep in as a qualification. In the early sixteenth century it is popularly said that Cardinal Wolsey, after he became Lord Chancellor, always had his black cat sitting beside his throne of justice, which turned out to mean good luck for some, bad for others.

As late as the seventeenth century, at the Feast of Taigheirm in Scotland, tradition called for a black cat to represent the demons of the underworld.

A jolly rebuttal to the bad luck superstition comes in the form of an old English folk rhyme:

> Whenever the cat of the house is black
> The lasses of lovers will have no lack.

Again, on the up side, black cats were a popular choice of sailors to bring good luck on their voyages, and the blacker the cat the better. In Yorkshire it was once claimed that a black cat brought good luck to the wife of a sailor, so long as she kept it in the house until her husband's return; meanwhile, if ever the cat escaped watch out for trouble at sea!

By the beginning of this century, the negative attitude toward the black cat would seem to have all but vanished, except to haunt us in the occasional horror film, rooted, perhaps, in Edgar Allen Poe's classic story. Poe's *The Black Cat* was illustrated with appropriate weirdness by Aubrey Beardsley in a special 1894–5 edition.

Affirmation of how the black cat had by now become accepted as a good omen came in a tobacco company's choice of 'Black Cat' as the brand name for its cigarettes. Far from being shunned by a superstitious public, Carrera's Black Cats during the 1920s became one of the most popular smokes in England.

It is often said that people either love or hate cats and that there's really no in-between. The suggestion has even been made that Shakespeare was one of the haters because his plays, written around the time 'when cat persecution became an obsession and cat killing a sport' reflect this attitude. But neither in Mercutio's reply to Tybalt (Tybalt, or Tybert, was also the name of the cat in the popular fifteenth century romance, *Reynard the Fox*) that he would like one of his nine lives, nor in Shylock's reference to 'a harmless and necessary cat' is there any indication of distrust, let alone dislike, by the author. Even the line 'some that are mad if they behold a cat' suggests that he himself wasn't such a person. Besides, had Shakespeare hated cats, he had every opportunity to degrade them by throwing one or two dark familiars on stage to add further shivers and shakes to the witches 'Double, double, toil and trouble' scene in *Macbeth*. Macbeth's own reference to a 'poor' cat suggests sympathy more than hate. And the First Witch in Act I, scene 1, merely alludes by name to her grey cat familiar, Graymalkin.

It is true that Shakespeare did not write a poem in praise of cats, as did Hardy, Christina Rossetti and Swinburne centuries later. But, partly because cats 'delight in silence, orderliness and peace' and partly because they were always the chosen pets of philosophers and writers, it is easy, somehow, to imagine a cat, a very intelligent-looking one, seated majestically at his feet as line after immortal line flowed from the master's pen. There is, of course, not one shred of evidence to support this idea, let alone a picture of Shakespeare with a cat.

Fifteenth and sixteenth century pictures of cats are, indeed, few and far between. Among these few are some woodcuts, showing, typically, a crude, heavy, greedy-looking creature almost always on the point of catching, clawing or chewing a mouse; their artists would appear to have had no particular fondness for cats. However, there is

Woodcut from *The Historie of Four-Footed Beastes* 1658

23

From the *Lincoln Bestiary*, 1150–1200 (Pierpoint Morgan Library)

Cat with mouse, unknown German artist c. 1500

one marvellous watercolour made by an Italian artist, Ulissi Aldrovandi, around 1580, which is reproduced here on pages 26–7.

It should be remembered that the enlightened Italy of the Renaissance escaped the Freya cult tragedy in northern Europe and that cats were generally smiled upon in ecclesiastical circles. They were the companion of several saints and occasionally found a place in a religious painting such as, for example, Dosso Dossi's early sixteenth century *Holy Family and Saints*. Leonardo da Vinci too made a preliminary pen and ink study for a 'Virgin and Child' canvas in which the child is drawn holding a cat. And in 1513, Leonardo also sketched some twenty cats on a single sheet which is now in England's Royal collection.

During the same century in Flanders, Pieter Breughel was becoming famous for his huge canvases crowded with people doing all manner of things: dancing, merry-making at a carnival, children playing games and, in *The Blue Cloak*, dated 1559, busily acting out popular proverbs. If you look long and hard enough at *The Blue Cloak* – the original is in Berlin's Gemäldegalerie – you will find a cat being belled, and quite obviously loathing every second of it.

Some fifty years later, Breughel's son, Jan, painted *The Garden of Eden* where, surely, the most beautiful animals this side of the Ark are seen lying down, as the prophet Isiah foretold, at peace with one another. (The painting is in the Victoria and Albert Museum, London.) The animals include tigers and lions; but not the domestic cat, who is nowhere mentioned in the Bible. In Albrecht Dürer's famous engraving of Adam and Eve, however (dated 1504), a domestic cat rests placidly at the foot of the apple tree and within two feet of an equally serene looking mouse. The two of them, along with the other animals, are, as in Breughel's Eden, obviously practising the art of peace.

In a most unusual sixteenth century portrait, *Sir Henry Wyat and his Cat*, the cat is given equal prominence to Sir Henry. The story behind it is particularly interesting. While still a young man, Henry Wyat was thrown into prison by King Richard III and tortured for siding with the Red Rose and Lancaster party in the raging Wars of

Woodcut from *The Ship of Fools*
by Sebastian Brant 1494
(Metropolitan Museum of Art,
New York)

OVERLEAF
Cat by Ulissi Aldrovandi,
Bologna, *c.* 1580

Felis alter syriacus punctis multis Insignitus.

Adam and Eve with animals,
Albrecht Dürer 1504

the Roses. There, in one of the darkest and worst dungeons, according to a report by Thomas Scott, young Wyat was saved from starving and freezing to death by a cat 'who one day came down into the dungeon unto him and as it were offered herself to him. Hee was glad of her, laid her in his bosome to warme him, and by making much of her, won her love: after this shee would come every day unto him, divers times, and when shee could gett one, bring him a pigeon.' The prisoner apparently struck a deal with the jailer who would dress and cook the birds. And so he managed to survive until he was freed by the new King, Henry VII, shortly thereafter to be awarded appointments at Court. From thenceforth Sir Henry, 'in his prosperity' it is said, 'would ever make much of a cat.'

From the seventeenth century onward there is an ever-increasing flow of cat stories, and splendid pictures too. Early examples include the work of the prolific Gottfried Mind, who became known in Switzerland as the 'Raphael of Cats'. Cornelis Visscher engraved *The Big Cat*, David Teniers pictured a *Cat Concert* and Gerard Dou a *Cat in Window*. In the eighteenth century A. F. Desportes was to make a wonderful gouache of *Kittens*, Jean-Baptiste Greuze included a poppet of a cat in *The Wool Winder*. So did François Drouais in his *Portrait of a Girl*, and Gainsborough painted a *Child with Cat*. By far the most reproduced cats in the history of painting, however, appear as details in two other eighteenth century portraits of children – one by Goya and the other by William Hogarth (pages 30 and 31).

In Hogarth's *The Graham Children*, the cat's tigerlike eyes focused on a bird cage and the dainty morsel perched within it are sufficiently hair-raising to scare any poor bird into a tailspin. The art critic, Sir Kenneth Clark, once remarked that the Graham children look hollow and lifeless beside her.

In Goya's portrait of the young Spanish nobleman, *Don Manuel Osorio de Zuniga*, the principal cat is a tortoiseshell who, with two companions, is staring hungrily at the pet magpie Don Manuel holds at the end of a long string. This cat, it has been aptly said, is the

28

possessor of 'the most purposeful-looking eyes in eighteenth century painting'.

Any discussion of the cat sooner or later returns to its eyes – which are featured in the illustrations on the next few pages. (Some artists claim that eyes are the hardest thing to get just right in a portrait, and it is not surprising therefore, that so many cat studies show the animal asleep or facing to one side, rather than head on).

In the first century Plutarch, looking at cats' eyes from a scientific point of view, observed how the pupils 'appear to grow full and dilate themselves at the full of the moon, but become thin and dull during the wane of that luminary'. W. B. Yeats was to say almost the same thing poetically in 'The Cat and the Moon':

> Does Minnaloushe know that his pupils
> Will pass from change to change,
> And that from round to crescent,
> From crescent to round they range?

A French scientist once referred to the cat as a 'lunatic beast', not meaning that it was odd or nutty – heaven forbid – but simply that it was influenced by the moon, possessing eyes which 'see clearly and gleam in the darkest nights'.

In the nineteenth century, Théophile Gautier wrote, 'A cat, with its phosphorescent eyes that stand it instead of lanterns, and sparks flashing from its back, moves fearlessly through the darkness where it meets wandering ghosts, witches, alchemists, necromancers, resurrectionists, lovers, thieves, murderers, grey-coated patrols and all other obscure larvae that emerge and work by night only.'

On a separate occasion, Gautier wrote movingly about the cat he loved so very much: 'Sometimes he will sit upon the carpet in front of you looking at you with eyes so melting, so caressing and so human, that they almost frighten you, for it is impossible to believe that a soul is not there'.

Virgin and Child with cat by Leonardo da Vinci (*British Museum*)

Pen drawing by
Leonardo da Vinci

29

LEFT
Detail from Goya's
*Don Manuel Osorio
Manrique de Zuniga*
© The Metropolitan
Museum of Art, The
Jules Bache Collection,
1949)

RIGHT
Cat gazing at a caged
bird. Detail from *The
Graham Children* by
William Hogarth (Tate
Gallery, London)

OVERLEAF
Cat's eyes. Photo:
Bruno Stefani

Mid 18C Whieldon-type
Staffordshire pottery cat
(The Manchester Collection)

RIGHT
Mother Cat with Three Kittens by
Gottfried Mind (detail)
(Oeffentliche Kunstsammlung,
Kupferstichkabinett Basel.
Photo: Hans Hinz)

T.-A. Steinlen

The Big Cat. Engraving by
Cornelis Visscher from *The Studio*

Cats and Dog (detail). Engraving
by Jan Griffier after Francis
Barton (The Cooper-Hewitt
Museum, The Smithsonian
Institution s National Museum of
Design, New York)

T.-A. Steinlen

Study of two kittens attrib. A.F. Desportes (Fitzwilliam Museum, Cambridge)

Wallpaper Fire Board. French,
19C (Courtesy of Cooper-Hewitt
Museum, New York, The
Smithsonian Institution's National
Museum of Design, Gift of
Marian Hague 1942–73–1)

RIGHT
Pottery cat, French, 19C
(Author's collection. Photo:
Charles Holme)

T.-A. Steinlen

OPPOSITE
Harem Life, Constantinople 1858
by John Frederick Lewis (Laing
Art Gallery, Newcastle-upon-
Tyne)

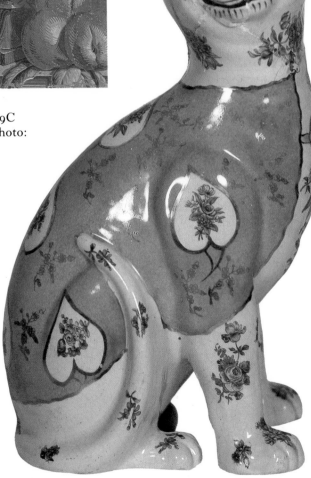

In the Orient, in China particularly, where the cat had been depicted as early as 2205 BC and where it was revered as the personification of the moon with occult powers enabling it to control tides and weather, it continued to be portrayed later, and beautifully so, as a household pet, frolicking in the gardens painted on silks and scrolls.

In Japan, where unknown centuries ago the cat had first been brought in from China, representations of the creature were quite similar to those of the Chinese, particularly and rather amusingly in the oriental look of the eyes. This was true in scroll paintings, many of which illustrated stories; as well as in pottery, bronzes and ivories.

Chinese porcelain cat night-lamp, 17–18C (Private collection)

RIGHT
Spring Play in a T'ang Garden, Chinese, 18C. Copy of a painting attributed to Hsuan Tsung (Metropolitan Museum of Art, New York, Fletcher Fund, 1947)

A few cats made their way into the Japanese print which, incidentally, was an aesthetic form that above all others was to make Japanese art popular in nineteenth century Europe, influencing Manet, Monet, Lautrec and other painters.

In the eighteenth century, Torii Kiyohiro and Kitagawa Utamaro were noted for prints that included cats; as were Andō Hiroshige and Kuniyoshi in the nineteenth century. Kuniyoshi loved to depict cats dressed as humans dancing at tea ceremonies, aping famous actors and, more realistically, stealing fish out of a bowl, playing with a ball of wool and chasing butterflies.

Cat up a tree. Chinese woodcut, 19C, artist unknown (Author's collection)

Cloisonné cat, Chinese, 16C (Private collection)

Japanese pottery cat, 20C
(Author's collection. Photo:
Charles Holme)

Cat with Butterfly, Chinese, 19C
(Author's collection)

Emma Homan
(*1842–1908*) by
John Bradley (©
The Metropolitan
Museum of Art, Gift
of Edgar William
and Bernice Chrysler
Garbisch, 1966.)

After looking at the subtle animal imagery found in most Oriental and Near Eastern brushwork, the art of nineteenth century Europe provides an interesting contrast in styles. The Victorians have been accused of over-sentimentalizing almost everything in their art. 'Pretty kitty' paintings and photographs were favourite subjects then, as they have remained ever since, for postcards, calendars and children's books. But after some of the ill-favoured early portraits of the cat the best of the pretty Victorian studies were a not unwelcome change. And the sweeter the fare, the more the cat world lapped it up.

Two Little Fraid Cats, Currier & Ives print, 19C

T.-A. Steinlen

RIGHT AND BELOW
Victorian Christmas cards

RIGHT
'Pretty kitty' postcard, 20C

OPPOSITE
'The Kittens' Wedding' (Potter's
Museum of Curiosity, Arundel,
Sussex)

46

RIGHT
'A Sleepy Place', unknown
photographer 1912 (Author's
collection)

BELOW
'On their Best Behaviour',
unknown photographer 1907
(Author's collection)

OPPOSITE
Siamese Kittens by Ylla, 1940s

MY BUT THIS IS A SLEEPY PLACE

Persian kittens, unknown
photographer *c.* 1910

'A Bundle of Mischief' (Author's
collection)

Three woodcuts from *Dame Wiggins of Lee and her Seven Wonderful Cats*; George Allen, 1885

From *A New Child's Play* by
E. V. B. (Eleanor Vere Boyle),
Sampson Low 1879

In so-called popular art, nothing changed much until well into the twentieth century when bombshells started to drop, not only in modern warfare but as venturesome artists like Picasso, Miró, Klee, to mention three who painted the occasional cat, helped to encourage a different, more abstract, way of looking at objects and the world around us.

The sudden abundance of cat literature and pictures in the nineteenth century was not only due to the renewed popularity of the cat, but to four of the many momentous inventions the Victorians brought about. One of these was the revolution in printing which transformed the manually operated press into an automatic power press capable of rolling out newspapers, magazines, prints and books by thousands

Study of a Cat by Théodore Géricault (Fogg Art Museum, Cambridge, Mass.)

Reclining white cat by Théodore Géricault (Ny Carlsberg Glyptotek, Copenhagen)

Seated cat, etching by Picasso, from *The Studio*

The Cats' Rendezvous, lithograph by Edouard Manet, from *The Studio*

rather than by tens, and at corresponding savings in cost. It was thus that the market for the less expensive story books, prints and reproductions of paintings widened, and with it the demand for good writers and artists to keep the publishers' lists active as well as to feed the hungry speed presses in the print shop.

The second remarkable breakthrough was the invention of the camera in the 1840s, which led to the continuing ascendancy of the art of photography. The third was the development of colour printing, brought about largely by the experiments of Edmund Evans in the 1860s. This advance transformed the crude penny-dreadful type of colour printing into one of subtle shades and textures, as seen, for example, in the Randolph Caldecott, Kate Greenaway and Arthur Rackham books.

Cat with frog by T.-A. Steinlen

RIGHT
Cat and fishbowl by T.-A. Steinlen

The hapless nymph with wonder saw:
A whisker first and then a claw.
   With many an ardent wish,
She stretched in vain to reach the prize.
What female heart can gold despise?
   What cat's averse to fish?
Oliver Goldsmith

OPPOSITE
'The Cats Have Come to Tea' by Kate Greenaway, from
The Marigold Garden, George Routledge & Son, 1885

White cat, 19C engraving by
Gustav Mutzel, from *The Studio*

OPPOSITE
Photo: Martin Munkacsi

The fourth nineteenth century innovation with far reaching effects
was the discovery in the 1880s of the photo-engraving reproduction
process. This made it possible for photographs (as opposite) to be
transferred directly onto the surface of a printing plate instead of, as
hitherto, undergoing the intermediary process of engraving the image
onto the plate by hand. The cat above was a hand engraving. Thus,
suddenly, instead of the unnatural photographic images seen in news-

'Mother with kittens', unknown German artist *c.* 1900 (Author's collection)

T.-A. Steinlen

'Surprise' by D. Merlin (Author's collection)

papers, magazines and books prior to the mid-1880s, the new continuous-tone reproductions showed all the subtle shades between light and dark, exactly as they were in the original picture. This discovery gave birth to art magazines like *The Studio* in 1893, which owed much of its success to its fine half-tone and colour reproductions, in addition to the subject matter itself. Many illustrations in this book, incidentally, come directly from *The Studio* and subsequent allied publications.

In the literature of the nineteenth century it was the French who really went overboard in eulogising the cat. English writers, on the whole, with notable exceptions such as Robert Southey, Charles Swinburne and Thomas Hardy, were looked down upon by the world of 'tail wavers' (*ailuroi*) as Herodotus called cats, for being altogether too chummy with dogs.

Théophile Gautier was a great friend of the even more noted ailurophile, Charles Pierre Baudelaire, whom he once described as 'a

Julie Manet and her Cat by Auguste Renoir
(Private collection)

voluptuous wheedling cat, with velvety manners'. Baudelaire simply adored cats 'which like himself are very fond of perfume and in whom the odour of valerian induces a sort of epileptic ecstasy'. Gautier also said that 'if a cat made its appearance at a door, or crossed a street', Baudelaire would always 'approach it, coax it to come to him, and then take it in his arms and pet it – sometimes stroking it the wrong way'.

One of the three poems from *Les Fleurs du Mal* which Baudelaire dedicated to his own cats, starts exquisitely with:

> Viens, mon beau chat, sur mon coeur amoreux;
> Retiens les griffes de ta patte,
> Et laisse-moi plonger dans tes beaux yeux,
> Mêlés de métal et d'agate.

Anatole France and Emile Zola managed to find ways of working their favourite pets into stories as did Colette in some of hers later. And yet another noted Frenchman whose heart beat faster when describing a cat was Honoré de Balzac – one of whose most brilliant pieces was a satire on the difference between the English and French approach to love-making as told by the cat Beauty, otherwise known as Minette, in *The Love Affairs of an English Cat*. The following is based on a translation by M. E. Jenkin.

Minette was brought up most decorously by her English spinster mistress who drilled into her the necessity of suffering 'a thousand deaths' rather than reveal her desires ... Thus 'deceived by appearances,' her mistress explained convincingly to Minette, 'everyone will take you for an angel'.

As Minette grows into a ravishing snow-white beauty, she is introduced to an aristocratic stuffed shirt of an Angora, handsome and 'black as night' named Puff who, through the will of her mistress, she becomes engaged to and eventually marries. Shortly thereafter, at a Temperance meeting the two are attending 'on the tiles', Minette decides that Puff is much 'too much of a politician to make a good husband'. As he nods off to sleep at the meeting, Minette is aroused by 'these delicious words' spoken by a young and nearly penniless tom named Brisquet from the French Embassy:

White kitten, C. E. Bullard

'Minette', illustration by J. I.
Grandville for Honoré de Balzac's
The Love Affairs of an English Cat

ABOVE AND BELOW
Illustrations by J. I. Grandville for
*Scenes from the Public and Private
Lives of the Animals*

OPPOSITE
'The Cat's Paw' by C. H. Bennett,
from *Bennett's Fables* (Pierpoint
Morgan Library)

'Dear Beauty,' says Brisquet caressingly: 'it will be long before Nature can produce a cat as perfect as you. The cashmeres of Persia and India are like the hides of a camel, compared with your fine and brilliant silk. You breathe a perfume to make Angels swoon with happiness ... The fire of your eyes lights up the night. Your ears would be perfection itself, if my sighs were to soften them. There is no rose in all England, which is as rosy as the rosy rim of your mouth ... Your paws carry softly and gracefully the body which epitomizes the miracles of the Creation; were it not surpassed by your tail, the elegant interpreter of your heart.'

Following this, and quite a few subsequent shall I's, shan't I's on the roof tops, and in the gutter, during which the drawbacks of love on a shoestring as opposed to life with a fat cat are pondered by Minette, she is prepared to elope with Brisquet when the two are discovered together, a scandal breaks out, Puff divorces Minette and Brisquet receives a bullet wound in his back, although, according to the 'revolting hypocrite of a Coroner,' as Minette describes him, he was found to have poisoned himself with arsenic. 'As if a tom, so gay, so crazy, so scatter-brained could ever have reflected on life long enough to have entertained such a serious idea', sobs Minette. 'How *could* a cat whom I loved ever have had the faintest desire to quit this life?'

The portrait of Minette, on page 63, is one of the splendid illustrations J. I. Grandville drew for Balzac's story. Through these and

Edward Lear's sketch of his cat, Foss

other similar and often funnier half-human, half-animal characters Grandville was to set a new trend which influenced many later artists including Charles H. Bennett, John Tenniel who, in 1865, illustrated Lewis Carroll's *Alice in Wonderland*, and Louis William Wain who specialized in cats and whose comic prints and cards are collectors items today. Louis Wain, H. G. Wells was to say, 'invented a cat style, a cat society, a whole cat world'. More accurately, Wain developed a cat style, a very amusing one, rather than invented it.

Other particularly renowned nineteenth century artists who loved and pictured cats were Théodore Géricault, Eugène Delacroix, Auguste Renoir, Edgar Degas, Toulouse-Lautrec, Edouard Manet, Gustav Mutzel, Edward Lear, Alexander Steinlen, Edward Penfield, and the American print makers, Currier and Ives, who included cats in their popular series of lithographs for framing. Many of the above are represented by pictures in these pages.

Probably the most famous of all cat stories is *Puss in Boots*, one of the oldest of fairy tales, in which the most cunning and eloquent of cats outsmarts everyone, including the fat ogre, in ways that enable him to present his young master, the nicest but poorest of a miller's three sons, not only with riches but with a castle and a title – the Marquess of Carabas – which more than qualify the handsome youth to claim the hand of the King's fair daughter.

The most familiar telling of *Puss in Boots* is by Charles Perrault, who based his 1697 version on an older Italian fairy tale which in turn probably came from a still earlier source.

Since the middle of the nineteenth century there have been countless reprints of Puss in collected fairy tales including special editions illustrated by various gifted artists, George Cruikshank included, but none have quite equalled the Gustave Doré engravings, one of which is reproduced here.

Puss in Boots was a natural choice for the English pantomime stage, vying for cat lovers' Christmas pocket money with the equally popular *Dick Whittington and His Cat*. But there was a difference. Puss was a fairy tale and Dick was for real. Had anyone dared suggest, as Dick

The Owl and the Pussy-Cat by
Edward Lear

The Owl and the Pussy-cat went to sea
   In a beautiful pea-green boat:
They took some honey, and plenty of money
   Wrapped up in a five-pound note.

Gustave Doré, illustration for
Perrault's *Puss in Boots*

T.-A. Steinlen

and his fanciful cat walked on stage to the customary round of applause, that the story probably wasn't true, there would likely have been such cat fits and hissings in the house that the safety curtain would have had to be rung down. So sacred are some traditions that no one wants to believe for a single minute that the cat which brought Dick fortune and fame wasn't a pussycat at all, but a kind of ketch popularly known as a 'cat' and used to haul coals from the Tyne to London. Apparently Whittington owned such a boat. Turning a deaf ear to this unromantic thought, the loyalists point out that Dick Whittington certainly did have a pet cat – a carved relief showing him with

67

Illustrations by Louis Wain (*c.* 1886)
below 'The Wrong Class' (postcard)
right, *above* 'Harmony', a print from the
collection of Mr and Mrs Harry Hildebrandt
far right 'Must we go?' (Author's collection)

right, *below* 'Family portrait'. Postcard,
unknown artist *c.* 1900

THE WRONG CLASS.

it was unearthed at Whittington's house in London – that he loved the cat, that the bells did ring out triumphantly, and that Dick was 'thrice Lord Mayor of London'. All of which is true as far as it goes; and so the legend prevails.

By comparison with Puss and Dick Whittington's cat, Williamina, the pet of the Dickens family, was unspectacular, down-to-earth and very real. Charles Dickens would never have turned cartwheels to own a cat, but he liked Williamina well enough, although, according to his daughter Mamie, he protested loudly when the cat, after giving birth to a family of kittens, transported them one by one from the kitchen to a corner of her choosing in his study. Dickens impatiently ordered Mamie to remove the kit and whole caboodle immediately. This she dutifully did. But Williamina was not a cat easily to be thwarted. She brought them back to the same corner of the study, and again they had to be taken away. The third time Williamina

Illustration for 'Dick Whittington' from *The Arthur Rackham Fairy Book* (courtesy Barbara Edwards, daughter of the artist)

Pantomime poster, *c.* 1900

70

decided it might be best to avoid this corner altogether and, placing the kittens at Dickens's feet, gave him 'such an imploring glance that he could resist no longer; and they were allowed to remain.'

Oswald Barron always wrote enchantingly of his cats, two of whom he had named James and Pippa. 'A slovenly cat was James, as ever I saw. Pippa, who will wash herself from ears to tail after eating the tail of a sardine, could never understand the fine carelessness of the male. I have seen her, in distress over his slovenliness, turn to and wash James and sleek out his fur. James bore her with humour; at such times his eye was like the eye of a man who is having his white tie properly tied for him by female hands.'

Illustration for 'The Cat that Walked by Itself' from *The Just So Stories* by Rudyard Kipling, Macmillan, London 1902

T.-A. Steinlen

In America, Mark Twain and Henry James loved their cats, and so, evidently, did Abraham Lincoln, who, according to General Horace Porter, 'once found three motherless cats in a tent in General Grant's camp and forthwith took them under his coat and, in the midst of the crushing cares of that awesome time, saw to it that they were cared for.'

Another American, President Theodore Roosevelt, was also known for his great partiality toward cats, one of which, no matter how many days or weeks he absented himself from his post at the White House 'never failed to turn up just before a big diplomatic dinner.' That prodigal is the hero of *Slippers, The White House Cat*, an account by Jacob A. Riis.

T.-A. Steinlen

71

BELOW AND OPPOSITE
'The Cats' Circus' by Louis Wain,
from *The Children's Tableaux*
(movable book) (Author's
collection)

The Cat by Z. Szalowska (Galerie
Naifs et Primitifs, New York and Paris)

Drawing by Beatrix Potter from *The Tale of the Pie and the Patty Pan*, Frederick Warne & Co., London

Two of the last great writers of the Victorian era were Charles Swinburne and Thomas Hardy. Swinburne's most famous poem begins sweetly and gently:

> Stately, kindly, lordly friend
> > Condescend
> Here to sit by me, and turn
> Glorious eyes that smile and burn,
> Golden eyes, love's lustrous meed,
> On the golden page I read.

And the first verse of Hardy's equally renowned tribute to his lately departed friend, which for years afterward he could never bring himself to replace, reads:

> Pet was never mourned as you,
> > Purrer of the spotless hue,
> Plumy tail, and wistful gaze
> > While you humoured our queer ways,
> Or outshrilled your morning call
> > Up the stairs and through the hall –
> Foot suspended in its fall –
> > While, expectant, you would stand
> Arched, to meet the stroking hand;
> > Till your way you chose to wend
> Yonder, to your tragic end.

Our own century is so rich with cat stories, drawings, paintings and photographs, it would take a whole book to do justice to a single decade. However, much of the best cat lore is so well known that mere mention of an author, illustrator or photographer is likely to recall a cherished memory, possibly of a book read in childhood such as one of Beatrix Potter's little gems.

Ever since Peter Rabbit stole through Mr McGregor's garden and

Young kitten. Photo W. Suschitzky

Photo: Elizabeth Hibbs

hopped into the hearts of Edwardian children, Peter and all the other animal tales Beatrix Potter wrote and illustrated have never ceased to be reached for by small and eager hands. Following the cat in *The Tale of the Pie and The Patty-Pan* in 1905 came *The Tale of Tom Kitten* who with Mittens and Moppet had 'dear little fur coats of

Mrs Ribby, from *The Tale of
Samuel Whiskers* by Beatrix
Potter, Frederick Warne & Co.,
London

RIGHT
Garden at Tenby, Wales by
Beatrix Potter (Victoria & Albert
Museum, London)

Felix the Cat. Pat Sullivan (King's Feature Syndicate)

Garfield. Jim Davis (© 1978 United Features Syndicate)

their own' and tails and whiskers which their mother, Mrs Tabitha Twitchit, combed. And soon after that, along came *The Story of Miss Moppet*.

Another early feline influence was the first film cartoon cat, Felix, who skipped and flickered his way along on celluloid to bring as much joy to the young of the 1920s as Sylvester did later and as Jim Davis's lazy, cynical, lasagne-loving Garfield does in the comic strip today.

The first quarter of the century saw a boom in handsome gift editions of the classics. Here the cat, usually in fairy tales or child's verses, was beautifully rendered by such illustrators as Eleanor Vere Boyle, Arthur Rackham, H. J. Ford, Edward J. Detmold, Heath Robinson, Edmund Dulac, Willy Pogany and Leslie Brooke.

Like Beatrix Potter's Tom Kitten and Ribby, a perennial nursery favourite is Tigger, the stuffed tiger cat in A. A. Milne's *The House at Pooh Corner*, who remains as alive today as when he first bounded across E. H. Shepard's drawing board in the 1920s.

In the adult world, one of the wittiest cat stories of all time is *Tobermory*, written by Hector Munro, better known as Saki.

Proof that Mr Cornelius Appin had worked miracles in teaching the cat Tobermory 'to speak our language with perfect correctness' was forthcoming when at Lady Blemley's house-party this 'Beyond-Cat' made his way 'with velvet tread and studied unconcern across to the group seated round the tea-table.'

Mavis Pellington, one of Lady Blemley's guests, asked the cat 'What do you think of human intelligence?' 'Of whose intelligence in particular?' asked Tobermory coldly.

'Oh, well, mine, for instance,' said Mavis with a feeble laugh.
'You put me in an embarrassing position,' said Tobermory, whose tone and attitude certainly did not suggest a shred of embarrassment.
'When your inclusion in this house party was suggested, Sir Wilfred protested that you were the most brainless woman of his acquaintance, and that there was a wide distinction between hospitality and the care of the feeble-minded. Lady Blemley replied that your lack of brain-

power was the precise quality which had earned you your invitation, as you were the only person she could think of who might be idiotic enough to buy their old car. You know, the one they call ''The Envy of Sisyphus'' because it goes quite nicely up-hill if you push it.'

And so the devastating satire proceeds to the expected unexpected Saki ending.

Another author as current as ever with his *Cats* is T. S. Eliot whose *Old Possum's Book of Practical Cats*, filled with poems originally intended merely to amuse his grandchildren, made its debut between hard covers in 1939. After numerous reprints, The Old Gumbie Cat, The Rum Tum Tugger, Mr Mistoffelees, Macavity, Skimbleshanks, Bustopher Jones and the Jellicle cats, come one and come all, accompanied by Andrew Lloyd Webber's music, first hit the London boards with velvety paws to thunderous bravos in 1981. The book was first illustrated by Nicolas Bentley, and more recently by Edward Gorey.

Cartoon by 'Boz', from *St Nicholas Magazine*, 1890

Illustration by Milt Gross for Margaret Linden's *Pasha the Persian*

OPPOSITE
Carter's Kittens, print
from The Carter Ink
Company (Private
collection)

Kitten by Clare Turlay Newberry (collection Molly Holme)

Drawing by C. G. Holme

81

LEFT
Illustration by Leonard
Leslie Brooke for 'The Owl
and the Pussy-Cat' from
*Nonsense Songs of Edward
Lear*, Frederick Warne &
Co., London

Walter de la Mare was another poet who was inspired to rhyme cats with rats, along with his 'Jekkel, and Jessop and one-eyed Jill' in *Five Eyes*. And W. H. Davies, to whom cats were

> .... strange, so strange
> I cannot sleep if one is near;
> And though I'm sure I see those eyes,
> I'm not so sure a body's there!

Orlando and Grace, from Kathleen Hale's *Orlando, His Silver Wedding*, Country Life Ltd, London 1944

Cat brooch (Author's collection)

Illustration by E. MacKinstry
for La Comtesse d'Aulnoy's
The White Cat, The Macmillan
Company, New York, 1928

84

'Dancing Cat', original lithograph
by Leonor Fini, from *La Grande
Parade des Chats*, Guillard,
Gourdon à Cachan (Author's
collection)

Annabelle by Jaye Holme 1984

Cats by Saul Steinberg (Private collection)

Drawing by Peggy Bacon

Paul Gallico was to surprise readers of *The Snow Goose* with his equally wonderful, but very different, *Jennie*, a fantasy about a little boy who became a cat, then once again with his description of his life with *My Boss The Cat* in which he tells what a great warm-up cats can be for a successful marriage.

They teach you your place in the household. The first thing kitty does is to organize your home on a comfortable basis – *her* basis. She'll eat when she wants to; she'll go out at her pleasure. She'll come in when she gets good and ready, if at all. She wants attention when she wants it and darned well means to be let alone when she has other things on her mind. She is jealous; she won't have you showering attention or caresses on any other minxes, whether two- or four-footed.

And so on through pages which, while telling how very trying the habits of cats can be at times, shows clearly how greatly Gallico has always enjoyed having them around.

Another literary treasure is publisher Michael Joseph's *Cat's Company*, published in 1947, an inside-out view of his and other people's cats with interesting real life stories; even advice on how to take care of your favourite pet.

P. G. Wodehouse in *The Story of Webster* jokes along with cats in the bar-parlour of the Anglers' Rest. 'The real objection to the great majority of cats', says a Mr Mulliner, with a shake of his head, 'is their insufferable air of superiority. Cats, as a class, have never completely got over the snootiness caused by the fact that in Ancient Egypt they were worshipped as gods. This makes them too prone to set themselves up as critics and censors of the frail and erring human beings whose lot they share.'

And it's always a joy to saunter down the garden path with Beverley Nichols. Talking of Oscar, Nichols points out in *Four, Five and Oscar* his trouble is 'simply one of an unfortunate environment in his youth. It is on a par with most juvenile delinquents who have come from unstable homes.... Oscar was actually encouraged in his naughtiness.

His original owner was a Chelsea artist who lived in a studio of quite exceptional squalor. Nothing was ever dusted, nothing was ever washed up ... In this excessively Bohemian atmosphere, where most of the furniture had been purchased off pavements ... and brought home on a barrow, Oscar could scratch to his heart's content. Shouts of laughter greeted his assaults as he tore the last few pieces of sackcloth off a chair with broken springs. And bets were taken on him when he began to climb the curtains.'

Cat Portraits, 1974, tempera, by Robert Vickrey (courtesy Midtown Galleries, New York)

Illustration from *The Elegant Beast*, by Leonard Lubin. Copyright © 1981 by Leonard Lubin. Reproduced by permission of Viking Penguin Inc.

Drawing by Ursula Landshoff (collection Yvonne McHarg)

OPPOSITE
'Happy Ending', pen and watercolour, by Ronald Searle (copyright © Ronald Searle 1974)

88

Returning to the world of junior books, which, after all, is where most animal stories with pictures customarily find their way into print, mention must certainly be made of Clare Newberry. Her enchanting illustrated stories of the 1930s and 1940s included *Mittens*, about a Persian kitten, and *Babette*, about a Siamese. Others on the long honour roll of Catland's Hall of Fame include, in the 1940s, Kathleen Hale with her classic *Orlando: the Marmalade Cat* illustrated stories, Feodor Rojankovsky for his cats in Elizabeth Coatsworths' *The Giant Golden Book of Cat Stories* and other books of the 1950s and 1960s. Barbara Cooney, Gustaf Tenggren, Wanda Gág, Vera Bock also drew the occasional wonderful cats along with other characters in children's books. Meg Wohlberg will be remembered for her illustrations for Eugene Field's *The Gingham Dog and The Calico Cat*.

More recently, Garth Williams must be singled out not only for his famous illustrations to Margery Sharpe's *Miss Bianca* stories, but also for his cat-with-mice gems all the way from George Selden's *The Cricket in Times Square*, in 1960, to his *Harry Cat's Pet Puppy* in 1974. Leonard Lubin included a most distinguished pair of cat croquet players in *The Elegant Beasts*, and Nicola Bayley, always noted for her pin-sharp renderings of cats, in 1984 came up with a wonderful series of books including *Parrot Cat* and *Polar Bear Cat*, in a size not much bigger than Beatrix Potter's.

In the art galleries, the drawings and reproductions of Gladys Emerson Cook's cats were popular, and so for a more sophisticated market was the work of the great Japanese-born Paris orientated artist, Foujita. Agnes Tait made lithographs of the cat, and there were those occasional and notable drawings by Alexander Calder, Peggy Bacon, Charles Sheeler and Andrew Wyeth, the sculptures of William Zorach and, more lately, the watercolours of Jaye Holme, the oils of Robert Vickrey and Robert Sivard, the lithographs of Virginia Miller and Guarnera, the unique painted stone cats of Susan French, and the fanciful lithographs of Leonor Fini, sixty of which were published in *La Grande Parade des Cats* (1973).

Illustration by F. Rojankovsky for *The Tall Book of Nursery Tales*,
©1944,1972, Western Publishing Co., Inc., Racine, WI

Nor, or course, can any art book fail to mention the genius Ronald Searle, who has been drawing deliciously outrageous cats for years – many, thankfully, to be shared by all in his various books. Equally unique are the illustrations of Tomi Ungerer and Edward Gorey which, like Searle's, clearly distinguish these bizarre cat-lovers cats from anyone else's.

Finally, while many world-renowned photographers have occasionally chosen to photograph the cat, masters like Edward Weston, John Rawlings, Werner Bischof, Martin Munkacsi, Nickolas Muray, Alfred Eisenstaedt, and others have always specialized in animal photography. Among the latter are Ylla, who took some of the most appealing pictures ever of kittens back in the 1930s, W. Suschitzky, who loved all animals and wrote the book *Photographing Animals*, Charles Phelps Cushing, Elizabeth Hibbs, Joseph R. Spies and Walter Chandoha, who has probably photographed more cats than anyone else in history.

So much is written about the aloofness of the cat, it would seem fitting to end this book with examples of how caring and loving cats can be towards humans. One example referred to earlier, was the cat that visited Sir Henry Wyat in his cell.

A similar story is told of Henry Wriothesley, third Earl of Southampton who, when imprisoned in the Tower of London, 'was surprised by a visit of his favourite cat, which had forced its way to the tower and reached his master by descending the chimney of his apartment.'

Lady Morgan told another story – of a beautiful and religious Italian peasant girl named Clementina, whose fits of epilepsy 'frequently struck her down to earth, in the midst of the village festival or church ceremony. If the saints, however, were negligent, Clementina had one friend whose vigilance never slumbered. It was her cat, which not only shared her bed, but followed her in her walks and devotions, from the vineyards to the altar.

'The first time Mina saw her mistress fall in a fit ... she exhibited the most extraordinary emotion.' And soon she was able to tell from

Illustration by Barbara Cooney for Margaret Wise Brown's *Where Have You Been?*, Hastings House Publishers, New York

Illustration by Garth Williams (©1974) for George Selden's *Harry Cat's Pet Puppy*, Farrar, Straus & Giroux Inc., New York

Mother and kitten. Painted stone by Susan French
(Author's collection. Photo: Charles Holme)

Cat, wood shavings
(Author's collection)

92

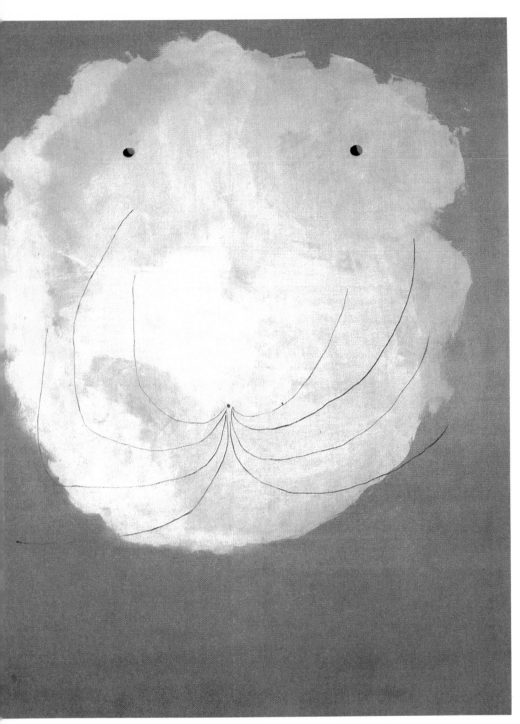

The Cat's Whiskers, Joan Mirò
(Private collection)

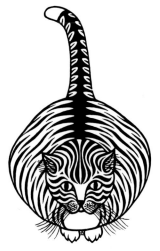

Tiger Cat. Woodcut by
Jacques Hnizdovsky (Private
collection)

93

Clementina's countenance when the affliction was about to hit, and would then run to the girl's parents, 'and by dragging their clothes, scratching at their persons, or mewing in the most melancholy manner' manage to get them to follow her to the fateful spot.

At fifteen the affliction brought Clementina to her tomb. The story continues:

Her cat walked after the bier, on which she was exposed as is the custom in Italy, and covered with flowers. During the funeral service she sat at the head of the bier, gazing with an intent look on the lifeless features of her young mistress; and when the grave was filling she made a vain endeavour to jump in, but was withheld by the bystanders who carried home this chief mourner after the . . . ceremony.

Mina, however, was seen the next morning stretched upon the new-made grave, which she continued to visit daily until she visited it for the last time; a few months after her friend's death she was found dead upon the green mound that covered her remains.

For one of the nicest tributes to a cat, we must turn back to Mohammed and his cat Muezza, and to Pierre Loti, the French naval officer and author whose real name was Julien Viand and of whom – with his cat – Henri Rousseau painted a famous portrait. Loti, who died in 1923 at the age of seventy-three, wrote most beautifully of his cats including, as Christabel Abercomay touchingly tells, 'a little Chinese slum cat who crept into his boat and would not be dislodged until, after months of lurking beneath his bed, she came out and crept into his heart.'

Of the prophet of Islam, Loti sat down to pen some of his most quoted lines: 'How well I can understand Mohammed, who in response to the chant of the muezzin summoning him to prayers, cut off with a pair of scissors the hem of his cloak before rising to his feet, for fear of disturbing his cat, which had settled down thereon to sleep.'

From *The Patchwork Cat*, by William Mayne, illustrated by Nicola Bayley. Illustration copyright © 1981 by Nicola Bayley. Reprinted by permission of Alfred A. Knopf, Inc. and Jonathan Cape Ltd

94

'Beauty'. Photo: Werner Bischof

Siamese cat by Clare Turlay
Newberry (Author's collection)

96